Loom Knit Baby Wraps

You'll be surprised how fast you can whip up a cozy afghan or cocoon for baby with these loom knit designs using chunky yarns or double strands of light weight yarn. Round and straight looms of various sizes are used, and skill levels range from Beginner to Intermediate.

LEISURE ARTS, INC. • Maumelle, Arkansas

Table of Contents

Meet Kathy Norris

Kathy Norris says her passion for fiber arts began more than 30 years ago when she first started knitting with needles. In recent years, she taught herself to use a knitting wheel (loom) while teaching at an arts and craft store. Her first loom knit designs were created to use in her classes to teach others how to use the loom. Now her designs can be found in various publications. In addition to knitting, she is a bead and crochet artist. Other Leisure Arts books and ebooks featuring Kathy's designs are *More Knitting Wheel Fashions* (#4411), *I Can't Believe I'm Loom Knitting* (#5250), *Big Book of Loom Knitting* (#5604), *Loom Knitting for Mommy and Me* (#5942), *Loom Knit Dishcloths* (#6369), *Big Book of Loom Knit Cowls* (#6611), and *Loom Knit Hats and Scarves* (#75471). For more about Kathy, visit KathyNorrisDesigns.com.

#5942

#6369

#6611

Rainbow Blocks

 **BEGINNER +**

Finished Measurement:

33" (84 cm) square

SHOPPING LIST

Yarn (Light Weight)

[3.5 ounces, 340 yards
(100 grams, 310 meters) per skein]:

- ☐ Red - 1 skein
- ☐ Light Yellow - 1 skein
- ☐ Yellow - 1 skein
- ☐ Green - 1 skein
- ☐ Orange - 1 skein
- ☐ Blue - 1 skein

Loom (round, large gauge)

- ☐ 30 Pegs

Additional Supplies

- ☐ Knitting loom tool
- ☐ Crochet hook, size J (6 mm)
- ☐ Yarn needle

This blanket is worked holding two strands of yarn together as one throughout. Roll each color into two balls **or** pull one strand from the center and one from the outside of the skein.

GAUGE INFORMATION

In Twisted Garter Stitch (e-wrap knit one row, purl one row), holding two strands of yarn together,

11 stitches and 22 rows = 4" (10 cm)
One Block = 11" (28 cm)

To skip 1 at the beginning of a row creates a finished look to the vertical edge. Place the working yarn **behind** the peg to be skipped.

INSTRUCTIONS

BLOCK (Make 9)

Working on the **inside** of the loom from **right** to **left**, holding two strands of Red together, and leaving a long end for sewing, chain cast on all 30 pegs *(Figs. 1a & b, page 28)*; work as flat knitting.

Row 1: Skip 1, e-wrap knit across.

Row 2: Skip 1, purl across.

Rows 3-10: Repeat Rows 1 and 2, 4 times.

To change colors, cut yarn leaving a long enough end to weave in later. Place the yarn end of the next color at the inside of the loom and begin working.

Repeat Rows 1 and 2, 5 times in each of the following colors: Light Yellow, Green, Orange, Blue, and Yellow.

Work chain one bind off across *(Figs. 6a-c, page 30)* leaving a long end for sewing.

ASSEMBLY

Using the Placement Diagram as a guide, sew the Blocks together using the long end left on the cast on or bind off edges.

PLACEMENT DIAGRAM

Quilt Star

 **EASY +**

Finished Measurement:
34" (86.5 cm) square

SHOPPING LIST

Yarn (Light Weight)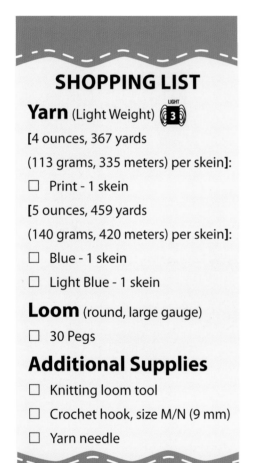

[4 ounces, 367 yards
(113 grams, 335 meters) per skein]:
☐ Print - 1 skein
[5 ounces, 459 yards
(140 grams, 420 meters) per skein]:
☐ Blue - 1 skein
☐ Light Blue - 1 skein

Loom (round, large gauge)
☐ 30 Pegs

Additional Supplies
☐ Knitting loom tool
☐ Crochet hook, size M/N (9 mm)
☐ Yarn needle

This blanket is worked holding two strands of yarn together as one throughout. Roll each color into two balls **or** pull one strand from the center and one from the outside of the skein.

GAUGE INFORMATION

In Twisted Stockinette Stitch (e-wrap knit each row), holding two strands of yarn together,

11 stitches and 15 rows = 4" (10 cm)
One Panel = 9" (22.75 cm) wide x
34" (86.5 cm) long

FOLLOWING A CHART

The diagonal sections are worked by following a chart. The chart shows each stitch as a square indicating what color each stitch should be. Visualize the chart as your fabric, beginning at the bottom edge. Follow the chart in the same direction as the row you are working.
For ease in following the chart, place a ruler on the chart **above** the row being worked to help keep your place.

To skip 1 at the beginning of a row creates a finished look to the vertical edge. Place the working yarn **behind** the peg to be skipped.

INSTRUCTIONS
RIGHT PANEL

Working on the **inside** of the loom from **right** to **left** and holding two strands of Print together, chain cast on 25 pegs (*Figs. 1a & b, page 28*); work as flat knitting.

Rows 1-32: Skip 1, e-wrap knit across.

To change colors when working with more than one color on each row, drop the color that you are working with to the inside of the loom. Then pick up the next color from beneath the strand of the old color (*Fig. 2a, page 28*). Do **not** cut yarn until instructed leaving a long enough end to weave in later.

Row 33: Skip 1, with Light Blue, e-wrap knit across.

Rows 34-64: Continuing to skip first peg of each row, follow Chart 1 Rows 2-32, using Light Blue for Color A and Print for Color B.

Cut Light Blue.

Rows 65-96: Continuing to skip first peg of each row, follow Chart 2 Rows 1-32, using Print for Color A and Blue for Color B.

Cut Blue.

Rows 97-128: With Print, skip 1, e-wrap knit across.

Work ▪◼▪ chain one bind off across *(Figs. 6a-c, page 30)* leaving a long end for sewing.

CENTER RIGHT PANEL

Working on the **outside** of the loom from **right** to **left** and holding two strands of Print together, chain cast on 25 pegs *(Fig. 1c, page 28)*; work as flat knitting.

Row 1: Skip 1, e-wrap knit across to last peg, with Blue, K1.

Rows 2-32: Continuing to skip first peg of each row, follow Chart 1 Rows 2-32, using Print for Color A and Blue for Color B.

Cut Print.

Rows 33-64: Continuing to skip first peg of each row, follow Chart 1 Rows 1-32, using Blue for Color A and Light Blue for Color B.

Rows 65-96: Continuing to skip first peg of each row, follow Chart 2 Rows 1-32, using Blue for Color A and Light Blue for Color B.

Cut Blue.

Rows 97-128: Continuing to skip first peg of each row, follow Chart 2 Rows 1-32, using Light Blue for Color A and Print for Color B.

Cut Light Blue.

Work chain one bind off across. The bind off can be worked with the inside of the loom facing you in order to work from right to left.

CENTER LEFT PANEL

Working on the **inside** of the loom from **right** to **left** and holding two strands of Print together, chain cast on 25 pegs; work as flat knitting.

Row 1: Skip 1, e-wrap knit across to last peg, with Light Blue, K1.

Rows 2-32: Continuing to skip first peg of each row, follow Chart 2 Rows 2-32, using Print for Color A and Light Blue for Color B.

Cut Print.

Rows 33-64: Continuing to skip first peg of each row, follow Chart 2 Rows 1-32, using Light Blue for Color A and Blue for Color B.

Rows 65-96: Continuing to skip first peg of each row, follow Chart 1 Rows 1-32, using Light Blue for Color A and Blue for Color B.

Cut Light Blue.

Rows 97-128: Continuing to skip first peg of each row, follow Chart 1 Rows 1-32, using Blue for Color A and Print for Color B.

Cut Blue.

Work chain one bind off across.

LEFT PANEL

Working on the **outside** of the loom from **right** to **left** and holding two strands of Print together, chain cast on 25 pegs; work as flat knitting.

Rows 1-32: Skip 1, e-wrap knit across.

Rows 33-64: Continuing to skip first peg of each row, follow Chart 2 Rows 1-32, using Blue for Color A and Print for Color B.

Cut Blue.

Rows 65-96: Continuing to skip first peg of each row, follow Chart 1 Rows 1-32, using Print for Color A and Light Blue for Color B.

Cut Light Blue.

Rows 97-128: Skip 1, with Print, e-wrap knit across.

Work chain one bind off across leaving a long end for sewing.

ASSEMBLY

Using the Placement Diagram as a guide and long ends, 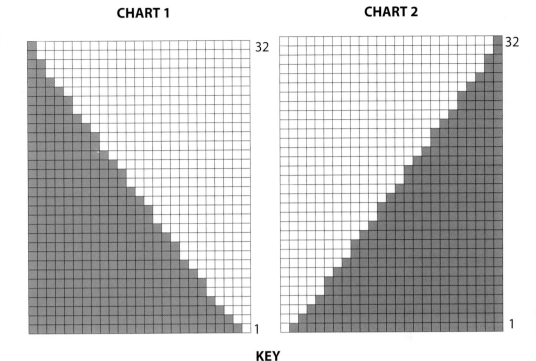 weave long edge of each side Panel to a corresponding Center Panel *(Fig. 7, page 30)*. Weave Center Panels together.

EDGING

With **right** side facing, using crochet hook, and holding 2 strands **each** of Light Blue and Blue together, place a slip knot on crochet hook, join yarn with slip stitch in any stitch on edge *(Fig. 11, page 31)*; slip stitch evenly around entire edge; join with slip st to first slip st, finish off.

CHART 1   **CHART 2**

32   32

1   1

KEY
■ - Color A
□ - Color B

PLACEMENT DIAGRAM

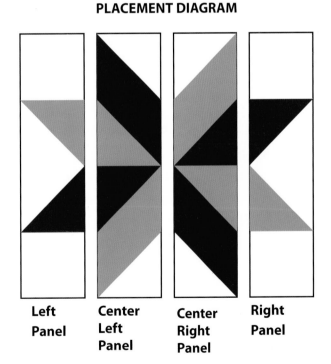

Left Panel   **Center Left Panel**   **Center Right Panel**   **Right Panel**

Bordered Square

 **BEGINNER**

Finished Measurement:
36" (91.5 cm) square

SHOPPING LIST

Yarn (Bulky Weight) **5 BULKY**
[3.5 ounces, 120 yards
(100 grams, 109 meters) per skein]:
☐ 6 skeins

Loom (straight, large gauge)
☐ 50 Pegs

Additional Supplies
☐ Knitting loom tool
☐ Crochet hook, size K (6.5 mm)
☐ Yarn needle

GAUGE INFORMATION

In Twisted Stockinette Stitch (e-wrap
knit each row),
 11 stitches and 17 rows = 4" (10 cm)
 One Panel = 18" (45.75 cm) wide

To skip 1 at the beginning of a row
creates a finished look to the vertical
edge. Place the working yarn **behind**
the peg to be skipped.

INSTRUCTIONS
RIGHT PANEL

Working on the **inside** of the loom
from **right** to **left**, chain cast on all
50 pegs *(Figs. 1a & b, page 28)*; work
as flat knitting.

Rows 1-6 (Bottom border): Skip 1, P1,
(EWK1, P1) across to last 2 pegs,
EWK2.

Row 7: Skip 1, P1, EWK1, P1, e-wrap
knit across.

Row 8: Skip 1, e-wrap knit across to
last 3 pegs, P1, EWK2.

First four stitches on the right edge of
the Panel form the side border.

Repeat Rows 7 and 8 for pattern until
Right Panel measures approximately
35" (89 cm) from cast on edge, ending
by working Row 8.

Last 6 Rows (Top border): Skip 1, P1,
(EWK1, P1) across to last 2 pegs,
EWK2.

Work chain one bind off across
(Figs. 6a-c, page 30) leaving a long
end for sewing.

LEFT PANEL

Working on the **inside** of the loom
from **right** to **left**, chain cast on
50 pegs and work as flat knitting.

Rows 1-6 (Bottom border): Skip 1, P1,
(EWK1, P1) across to last 2 pegs, EWK2.

Row 7: Skip 1, e-wrap knit across to
last 3 pegs, P1, EWK2.

Row 8: Skip 1, P1, EWK1, P1, e-wrap
knit across.

First four stitches on the left edge of
the Panel form the side border.

Repeat Rows 7 and 8 for pattern until
Left Panel measures approximately
35" (89 cm) from cast on edge, ending
by working Row 8.

Last 6 Rows (Top border): Skip 1, P1,
(EWK1, P1) across to last 2 pegs, EWK2.

Work chain one bind off across.

ASSEMBLY

Weave long edges of Panels
together, placing side borders at
outer edges *(Fig. 7, page 30)*.

Basketweave

 BEGINNER

Finished Measurement:

34½" x 34" (87.5 cm x 83 cm)

SHOPPING LIST

Yarn (Light Weight) 🧶

[5 ounces, 459 yards
(140 grams, 420 meters) per skein]:

☐ 4 skeins

Loom (straight, large gauge)

☐ 62 Pegs

Additional Supplies

☐ Knitting loom tool

☐ Crochet hook, size J (6 mm)

☐ Yarn needle

This blanket is worked holding two strands of yarn together as one throughout.

GAUGE INFORMATION

In pattern, holding two strands of yarn together,

2 repeats (12 stitches) = 3½" (9 cm)
2 repeats (24 rows) = 4" (10 cm)
One Panel = 17½" (44.5 cm) wide x 34" (83 cm) long

INSTRUCTIONS
RIGHT PANEL
BOTTOM BORDER

Working on the **inside** of the loom from **right** to **left** and holding two strands together, 🎥 chain cast on 60 pegs (*Figs. 1a & b, page 28*); work as flat knitting.

Row 1: Purl across.

Row 2: Knit across.

Rows 3-9: Repeat Rows 1 and 2, 3 times; then repeat Row 1 once **more**.

BODY

First five stitches on the right edge of the Panel form the side border.

Row 1: K1, P4, (K2, P4) across to last 7 pegs, K7.

Row 2: P5, knit across.

Row 3: K1, P4, (K2, P4) across to last 7 pegs, K7.

Row 4: P5, knit across.

Row 5: Knit across.

Row 6: P5, knit across.

Row 7: K1, P1, K2, (P4, K2) across to last 8 pegs, P3, K5.

Row 8: P5, knit across.

Row 9: K1, P1, K2, (P4, K2) across to last 8 pegs, P3, K5.

Row 10: P5, knit across.

Row 11: Knit across.

Row 12: P5, knit across.

Repeat Rows 1-12 for pattern until Right Panel measures approximately 32¾" (83 cm) from cast on edge, ending by working Row 9.

Row 4: Knit across to last 5 pegs, P5.

Row 4: Knit across to last 5 pegs, P5.

Row 5: Knit across.

Row 6: Knit across to last 5 pegs, P5.

Row 7: K5, P1, K2, (P4, K2) across to last 4 pegs, P3, K1.

Row 8: Knit across to last 5 pegs, P5.

Row 9: K5, P1, K2, (P4, K2) across to last 4 pegs, P3, K1.

Row 10: Knit across to last 5 pegs, P5.

Row 11: Knit across.

Row 12: Knit across to last 5 pegs, P5.

Repeat Rows 1-12 for pattern until Left Panel measures approximately 32¾" (83 cm) from cast on edge, ending by working Row 9.

TOP BORDER
Rows 1-9: Work same as Bottom Border.

Work chain one bind off across leaving a long end for sewing.

ASSEMBLY
Weave long edges of Panels together, placing side borders at outer edges and being careful to match pattern rows *(Fig. 7, page 30)*.

TOP BORDER
Row 1: Purl across.

Row 2: Knit across.

Rows 3-9: Repeat Rows 1 and 2, 3 times; then repeat Row 1 once **more**.

Work chain one bind off **across** *(Figs. 6a-c, page 30)*. The bind off can be worked with the inside of the loom facing you in order to work from right to left.

LEFT PANEL
BOTTOM BORDER
Working on the **inside** of the loom from **right** to **left** and holding two strands together, chain cast on 60 pegs; work as flat knitting.

Row 1: Purl across.

Row 2: Knit across.

Rows 3-9: Repeat Rows 1 and 2, 3 times; then repeat Row 1 once **more**.

BODY
First five stitches on the left edge of the Panel form the side border.

Row 1: K5, P4, (K2, P4) across to last 3 pegs, K3.

Row 2: Knit across to last 5 pegs, P5.

Row 3: K5, P4, (K2, P4) across to last 3 pegs, K3.

Ripples

Shown on page 17.

 **INTERMEDIATE**

Finished Measurement:
33½" x 35½" (85 cm x 90 cm)

SHOPPING LIST

Yarn (Light Weight) 🧶 **③**
[1.75 ounces, 161 yards
(50 grams, 147 meters) per skein]:
☐ Yellow - 5 skeins
☐ Light Yellow - 5 skeins

Loom (Straight, large gauge)
☐ 62 Pegs

Additional Supplies
☐ Knitting loom tool
☐ Crochet hook, size J (6 mm)
☐ Yarn needle

This blanket is worked holding two strands of yarn together as one throughout. Either use one strand from each of two skeins, **or** one skein pulling one strand from the center and one from the outside of the skein.

GAUGE INFORMATION
In ripple pattern, holding two strands of yarn together,
One repeat (10 stitches) and
16 rows = 3" (7.5 cm)
One Panel = 17" (43.25 cm) wide

INSTRUCTIONS
RIGHT PANEL
BOTTOM BORDER
Working on the **inside** of the loom from **right** to **left** and holding two strands of Yellow together, 🎥 chain cast on 57 pegs *(Figs. 1a & b, page 28);* work as flat knitting.

Row 1: Knit across.

Row 2: Purl across.

Rows 3 and 4: Repeat Rows 1 and 2.

BODY
The ripple pattern is made by alternating 2 rows of each color, without cutting the yarn. Drop Yellow to the inside of the loom and begin using 2 strands of Light Yellow, leaving a long end to weave in later. Twist the yarns at the end of every other row when 🎥 changing colors *(Fig. 2b, page 28).*

First six stitches on the right edge of the Panel form the side border.

Row 1: With Light Yellow, knit across.

Row 2: Purl across.

Row 3 (Eyelet row):
First, set up for the decreases beginning at the right edge. Move the loop from the eleventh peg to the twelfth peg, ★ skip next 8 pegs, and move the loop from the next peg to the peg on the left; repeat from ★ 3 times **more**.

Then, work the row beginning at the right edge. With Yellow, K6, ★ † beginning with the peg before the empty peg, move the loops from the next 4 pegs one at a time to an empty peg (**Fig. A**), creating a new empty peg, e-wrap empty peg, K3, skip 1 with yarn in **back**, knit next peg lifting the bottom 2 loops over the working yarn and off the peg. Move the loop just made to the skipped peg. Without knitting it, lift the bottom loop over the top loop and off the peg, move the loops from the next 3 pegs one at a time to the right, K3, e-wrap next peg †, K1; repeat from ★ 3 times **more**, then repeat from † to † once, K2.

Fig. A

Row 4: Knit across to last 6 pegs, P6.

Repeat Rows 1-4 for pattern until Right Panel measures approximately 34" (86.5 cm) from cast on edge, ending by working Row 2.

Cut Light Yellow.

TOP BORDER
Rows 1-4: With Yellow, work same as Bottom Border.

Work 🎥 chain one bind off across (**Figs. 6a-c, page 30**).

LEFT PANEL
BOTTOM BORDER
Work same as Right Panel.

BODY
First six stitches on the left edge of the Panel form the side border.

Row 1: With Light Yellow, knit across.

Row 2: Purl across.

Row 3 (Eyelet row):
First, set up for the decreases beginning at the right edge. Move the loop from the sixth peg to the seventh peg, ★ skip next 8 pegs, and move the loop from the next peg to the peg on the left; repeat from ★ 3 times **more**.

Then, work the row beginning at the right edge. With Yellow, K1, ★ † beginning with the peg before the empty peg, move the loops from the next 4 pegs one at a time to an empty peg, creating a new empty peg, e-wrap empty peg, K3, skip 1 with yarn in **back**, knit next peg lifting the bottom 2 loops over the working yarn and off the peg. Move the loop just made to the skipped peg. Without knitting it, lift the bottom loop over the top loop and off the peg, move the loops from the next 3 pegs one at a time to the right, K3, e-wrap next peg †, K1; repeat from ★ 3 times **more**, then repeat from † to † once, K6.

Row 4: P6, knit across.

Repeat Rows 1-4 for pattern until Left Panel has the same number of Light Yellow ridges as Right Panel, ending by working Row 2.

TOP BORDER
Rows 1-4: With Yellow, work same as Right Panel Bottom Border.

Work chain one bind off across leaving a long end for sewing.

🎥 Weave long edges of Panels together, placing side borders at outer edges and being careful to match pattern rows (**Fig. 7, page 30**).

Hexagons

 **INTERMEDIATE**

Finished Measurement:
35" (89 cm) long

SHOPPING LIST

Yarn (Light Weight) 〔3〕
[5 ounces, 459 yards
(140 grams, 420 meters) per skein]:
☐ Pink - 1 skein
☐ Yellow - 1 skein
☐ Green - 1 skein

Loom (round, extra-large gauge)
☐ 36 Pegs

Additional Supplies
☐ Knitting loom tool
☐ Crochet hook, size J (6 mm)
☐ Yarn needle

This blanket is worked holding two strands of yarn together as one throughout. Roll each color into two balls or pull one strand from the center and one from the outside of the skein.

GAUGE INFORMATION

In Twisted Garter Stitch (e-wrap knit one row, purl one row), holding two strands of yarn together,

> One Motif = 7" (17.75 cm) from side to side

INSTRUCTIONS

Each Motif is made by using short rows to form the corners.

🎥 Short rows are formed by only working across some of the pegs before stopping and working back. When instructed to turn, change the direction you are working. This method adds extra length to some of the stitches to form a corner.

MOTIF A (Make 13)

Work a 🎥 gathered cast on as follows: Holding two strands of Pink together, anchor the yarn with a slip knot; working from **left** to **right**, weave around all 36 pegs, placing yarn behind first peg, in front of next peg, (behind next peg, in front of next peg) around (*Fig. A*).

Fig. A

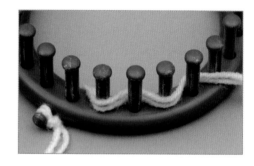

Working as circular knitting, ★ skip next peg placing yarn in front of peg, e-wrap knit next peg (*Fig. B*); repeat from ★ around.

Fig. B

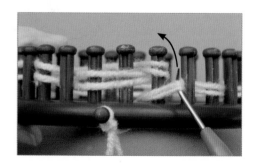

Rnds 1-3: (P1, EWK1) around.

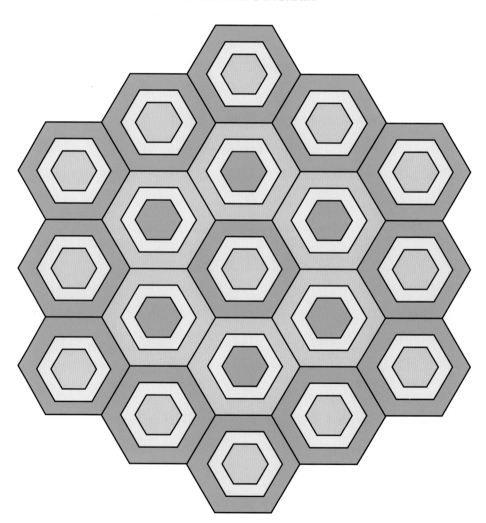

To change colors, cut yarn leaving a long enough end to weave in later. Place the yarn end of the next color at the inside of the loom and begin working.

Rnd 4: With Yellow, EWK6, ★ wrap next peg *(Figs. 3a & b, page 29)*; turn, EWK1, wrap next peg; turn; EWK1, e-wrap knit wrapped peg (lifting **both** loops over the top loop and off the peg), EWK5; repeat from ★ around, wrap first peg; turn, EWK1, wrap next peg; turn, EWK1.

Rnds 5 and 6: Continuing to e-wrap the wrapped stitches, EWK6, ★ wrap next peg; turn, EWK1, wrap next peg; turn; EWK7; repeat from ★ around, wrap first peg; turn, EWK1, wrap next peg; turn, EWK1.

Cut Yellow.

Rnd 7: With Green, repeat Rnd 5.

Rnd 8: P6, ★ wrap next peg; turn, EWK1, wrap next peg; turn; P7; repeat from ★ around, wrap first peg; turn, EWK1, wrap next peg; turn, EWK1.

Rnd 9: With Green, repeat Rnd 5.

Rnd 10: Repeat Rnd 8.

Rnd 11: Loosely e-wrap knit around.

Loosely work chain one bind off around *(Figs. 6a-c, page 30)*.

Pull beginning end to close Motif; secure end.

MOTIF B (Make 6)
Beginning with Green, work same as Motif A working Rnds 7-11 with Pink.

ASSEMBLY

Using the Placement Diagram as a guide, sew the Motifs together using matching colors forming strips; then sew strips together.

PLACEMENT DIAGRAM

Bunny Cocoon & Hat

 **EASY**

Finished Measurements:

Cocoon: 20" long x 24" circumference (51 cm x 61 cm)

Hat: 13" (33 cm) circumference

SHOPPING LIST

Yarn

Cocoon & Hat Ears:

(Bulky Weight)

[1.76 ounces, 63 yards (50 grams, 57 meters) per skein]:

☐ 2 skeins

Hat Only:

(Medium Weight) 4

[5 ounces, 256 yards (141 grams, 234 meters) per skein]:

☐ 1 skein

Loom (round)

☐ **Cocoon** - 40 Pegs (extra-large gauge)

☐ **Hat** - 30 Pegs (large gauge)

Additional Supplies

☐ Knitting loom tool

☐ Crochet hook, size K (6.5 mm)

☐ Yarn needle

The main portion of the Hat is worked holding two strands of medium weight yarn together as one. Roll yarn into two balls **or** pull one strand from the center and one from the outside of the skein.

GAUGE INFORMATION

In Twisted Stockinette Stitch (e-wrap knit each row),

Cocoon

With bulky weight yarn,

7 stitches and 12 rows = 4¼" (10.75 cm)

Hat

With medium weight yarn, holding two strands of yarn together,

7 stitches and 11 rows = 3" (7.5 cm)

INSTRUCTIONS
COCOON

Working on the **inside** of the loom from **right** to **left**, using bulky weight yarn, 📹 chain cast on all 40 pegs *(Figs. 1a & b, page 28)*; work circularly.

Rnd 1: E-wrap knit around.

Rnd 2: Purl around.

Rnds 3 and 4: Repeat Rnds 1 and 2.

E-wrap knit each stitch until Cocoon measures approximately 20" (51 cm) from cast on edge.

Cut yarn leaving a 40" (101.5 cm) length for sewing. Thread a yarn needle with the yarn end.

To work 📹 gathered removal, begin with the last peg worked and insert the yarn needle in each loop from **bottom** to **top** *(Fig. A)* lifting them off the pegs and sliding them onto the yarn end. With the yarn end to the **wrong** side of the piece, pull the end to gather the loops; secure end *(Fig. B)*.

Fig. A

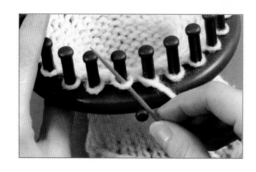

Fig. B

HAT

Working on the **inside** of the loom from **right** to **left**, holding two strands of medium weight yarn together, chain cast on all 30 pegs; work circularly.

Rnd 1: E-wrap knit around.

Rnd 2: Purl around.

Rnds 3-6: Repeat Rnds 1 and 2 twice.

E-wrap knit each stitch until Hat measures approximately 5" (12.5 cm) from cast on edge.

Cut yarn leaving a 30" (76 cm) length for sewing. Thread a yarn needle with the yarn end.

Work gathered removal *(Figs. A & B)*.

EAR (Make 2)

Using bulky weight yarn, e-wrap cast on 6 pegs from **left** to **right**; holding two strands of medium weight yarn together, cast on 3 pegs: 9 pegs.

📹 To change colors when working with more than one color on each row, drop the color that you are working with to the inside of the loom. Then pick up the next color from underneath the strand *(Fig. 2a, page 28)*.

Rows 1-10: Using matching color, e-wrap knit each peg.

As decreases are formed, move stitches as needed to eliminate skipped pegs.

Row 11: Using medium weight yarn, EWK1,  left e-wrap decrease *(Figs. 4a & b, page 29)*, using bulky weight yarn, left e-wrap decrease 3 times: 5 pegs remaining.

Row 12: Using bulky weight yarn, EWK1, left e-wrap decrease, cut bulky weight yarn; using medium weight yarn, left e-wrap decrease: 3 pegs remaining.

Row 13: Move loop from second peg to first peg, then move loop from third peg to first peg, e-wrap knit first peg lifting all 3 loops over top loop; cut yarn leaving a long end for sewing, pull end through loop.

Fold Ear in half matching rows; weave edges together *(Fig. 7, page 30)*, then sew Ear to top of Hat.

Hooded Cocoon

 **EASY**

Finished Measurement:

30" long x 23" circumference
(76 cm x 58.5 cm)

SHOPPING LIST

Yarn (Super Bulky Weight) **6**

[10.5 ounces, 220 yards
(300 grams, 201 meters) per skein]:

☐ 1 skein

Loom (round, extra-large gauge)

☐ 40 Pegs

Additional Supplies

☐ Knitting loom tool
☐ Crochet hook, size L (8 mm)
☐ Yarn needle

GAUGE INFORMATION

In Twisted Stockinette Stitch (e-wrap knit each row),

7 stitches and 11 rows = 4" (10 cm)

INSTRUCTIONS
BODY

Working on the **inside** of the loom from **right** to **left**, chain cast on all 40 pegs **(Figs. 1a & b, page 28)**; work circularly.

Rnd 1: E-wrap knit around.

Rnd 2 (Eyelet rnd): ★ Left e-wrap decrease **(Figs. 4a & b, page 29)**, e-wrap empty peg; repeat from ★ around.

E-wrap knit each stitch until Cocoon measures approximately 20" (51 cm) from cast on edge.

HOOD

Begin working as flat knitting.

Row 1: Working from **right** to **left**, EWK1, left purl decrease **(Figs. 5a & b, page 29)**, EWK1, P1, e-wrap knit around to last 5 pegs, P1, EWK1, left purl decrease, EWK1: 38 pegs remaining.

As decreases are formed, move stitches as needed to eliminate skipped pegs.

To skip 1 at the beginning of a row creates a finished look to the vertical edge. Place the working yarn **behind** the peg to be skipped.

Rows 2-5: Skip 1, left purl decrease, EWK1, P1, e-wrap knit across to last 5 pegs, P1, EWK1, left purl decrease, EWK1: 30 pegs remaining.

Row 6: Skip 1, P1, EWK1, P1, e-wrap knit across to last 4 pegs, P1, EWK1, P1, EWK1.

Repeat Row 6 until Hood measures approximately 10" (25.5 cm), ending with working yarn on the right-hand edge.

Work  chain one bind off across *(Figs. 6a-c, page 30)* leaving a long end for sewing.

Fold Hood in half matching bound off stitches; sew stitches together.

TIE

Working on the **inside** of the loom from **right** to **left**, chain cast on 3 pegs.

Work 🎥 3 stitch I-cord as follows:

★ Working as circular knitting, bring the working yarn across the inside of the loom, then outside to the left of the first peg that was worked *(Fig. A)*. Working from **left** to **right**, e-wrap knit the 3 pegs; repeat from ★ for I-cord until Tie measures approximately 35" (89 cm), giving the cord a tug every few rnds to close the gap between the first and last stitches *(Fig. B)*; cut yarn and pull end through loop.

Beginning at center front, weave Tie through eyelets on Row 2 of Body.

Fig. A

Fig. B

ABBREVIATIONS

cm	centimeters
EWK	e-wrap knit
K	knit
mm	millimeters
P	purl
Rnd(s)	Round(s)

SYMBOLS & TERMS

★ — work instructions following ★ as many **more** times as indicated in addition to the first time.

† to † — work all instructions from first † to second † **as many** times as specified.

( ) or [ ] — work enclosed instructions **as many** times as specified by the number immediately following **or** contains explanatory remarks.

colon (:) — the number(s) given after a colon at the end of a row or round denote(s) the number of of pegs you should have occupied at the end of that row or round.

working yarn — the strand coming from the skein.

GAUGE

Gauge is the number of stitches and rows or rounds in every inch of your knitting and is used to control the finished size.

Exact gauge is essential for proper size. Before beginning your project, make a sample swatch approximately 4" (10 cm) wide with the yarn and loom specified in the individual instructions. After completing the swatch, give it a tug, holding the cast on and bound off edges, then let it "rest."

Measure it, counting your stitches and rows carefully. If your swatch is larger or smaller than specified, make another, changing your tension of the working yarn as you form the stitches. Keep trying until you find the tension you need to achieve gauge. Maintain established gauge throughout project.

Yarn Weight Symbol & Names	SUPER FINE 1	FINE 2	LIGHT 3	MEDIUM 4	BULKY 5	SUPER BULKY 6	JUMBO 7
Type of Yarns in Category	Sock, Fingering, Baby	Sport, Baby	DK, Light Worsted	Worsted, Afghan, Aran	Chunky, Craft, Rug	Bulky, Roving	Jumbo, Roving

■□□□ BEGINNER		Projects for first-time loom knitters using basic knit and purl stitches, and simple color changes.
■■□□ EASY		Projects using basic stitches, repetitive stitch patterns, simple color changes, and simple shaping and finishing.
■■□□ EASY +		Projects using basic stitches, repetitive stitch patterns, simple color changes, simple short rows, and simple shaping and finishing.
■■■□ INTERMEDIATE		Projects with a variety of stitches, such as lace, also short rows, and mid-level shaping and finishing.

CHAIN CAST ON

Leaving a 6" (15 cm) end, make a slip knot (*Figs. 8a-c, page 31*), placing it on the crochet hook.

★ Working on the **inside** of the loom, you will cast on from **right** to **left**. Wrap the working yarn around the outside of the peg and bring it to the inside. Lay the working yarn on top of the crochet hook with the peg being encircled by the yarn. Catching the working yarn with the hook, bring it through the loop on the hook (*Fig. 1a*), producing a chain stitch with the peg in the middle of the chain stitch.

Fig. 1a

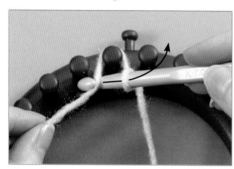

Repeat from ★ until you have cast on all but one peg needed.

For the last cast on stitch, keep the working yarn to the inside of the loom and place the loop from the hook onto the next empty peg (*Fig. 1b*). Turn the loom to work on the outside.

Fig. 1b

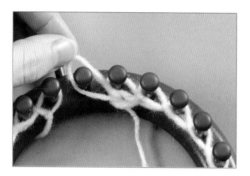

Note: To chain cast on working on the **outside** of the loom, from **left** to **right**. hold the working yarn and crochet hook inside the loom. Work the same as before, only wrapping the yarn around the outside of the pegs (*Fig. 1c*).

Fig. 1c

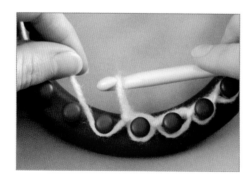

CHANGING COLORS

The first time the second color is used, drop the color that you are using to the inside of the loom and begin working with the new color leaving a long end to weave in later.

To change colors, drop the color that you are working with to the inside of the loom. Then pick up the next color from underneath the strand (*Fig. 2a or b*). This will twist the yarns to prevent holes when working a color pattern, or create a neat edge when working in stripes. Do **not** cut the yarn unless specified.

Fig. 2a

Fig. 2b

WRAPPING THE PEG

In order to prevent holes when working short rows, it is necessary to wrap the yarn around an unworked peg before changing directions.

Work across the pegs indicated in the pattern. Wrap the next peg as follows:

Step 1: Using the tool, lift the loop from the peg to be wrapped and hold it on the tool.

Step 2: Bring the working yarn behind the empty peg, then to the outside of the loom and across the front of the empty peg *(Fig. 3a)*.

Fig. 3a

Step 3: Put the loop back onto the peg. The wrap will be under the loop *(Fig. 3b)*.

Fig. 3b

Bring the working yarn back to the inside of the loom so that it is in position to work back in the other direction, leaving the remaining pegs unworked.

DECREASES
LEFT E-WRAP DECREASE

Use the tool to move the loop from peg A to the **left** and place it on peg B, leaving peg A empty *(Fig. 4a)*. E-wrap knit peg B *(Fig. 4b)* working both strands as one.

Fig. 4a

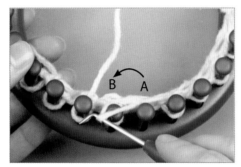

Fig. 4b

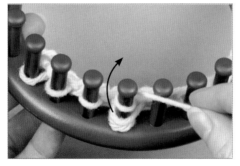

LEFT PURL DECREASE

Use the tool to move the loop from peg A to the **left** and place it on peg B, leaving peg A empty *(Fig. 5a)*. Purl peg B working both strands as one *(Fig. 5b)*.

Fig. 5a

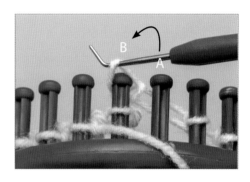

Fig. 5b

CHAIN ONE BIND OFF

With the working yarn to the inside of the loom, insert a crochet hook in the loop on the last peg worked, from **bottom** to **top**, and lift it off the peg. To chain 1, lay the working yarn on top of the crochet hook and bring it through the loop on the hook *(Fig. 6a)*, insert the hook in the loop on the next peg, from **bottom** to **top**, lift it off the peg and pull it through the loop on the hook *(Fig. 6b)*.

Fig. 6a

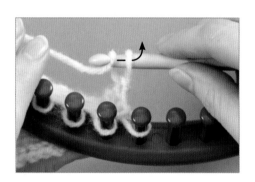

Fig. 6b

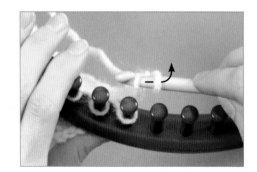

★ Chain 1, insert the hook in the loop on the next peg, from **bottom** to **top**, lift it off the peg and pull it through the loop on the hook; repeat from ★ until all of the loops have been removed from the loom and there is one loop left on the crochet hook. Chain 1, cut the yarn and pull the end through the final loop *(Fig. 6c)*; tighten the loop.

Fig. 6c

Note: If the last row was worked from right to left, you will need to hold the loom with the inner edge facing while binding off.

WEAVING SEAMS

With the **right** side of both pieces facing you and edges even, sew through both sides once to secure the seam. Insert the needle under the bar between the first and second stitches on the row and pull the yarn through *(Fig. 7)*. Insert the needle under the next bar on the second side. Repeat from side to side, being careful to match rows. If the edges are different lengths, it may be necessary to insert the needle under two bars at one edge.

Fig. 7

BASIC CROCHET STITCHES
SLIP KNOT

Make a circle and place the working yarn under the circle *(Fig. 8a)*. Either pick up the bar with your fingers and place it on the side peg of the loom, pulling the loose end of the yarn to tighten the slip knot, **or** insert a crochet hook under the bar just made *(Fig. 8b)* and pull the loose end of the yarn to complete the slip knot forming a loop *(Fig. 8c)*.

Fig. 8a

Fig. 8b

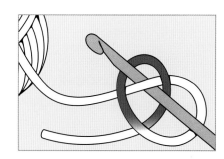

Fig. 8c

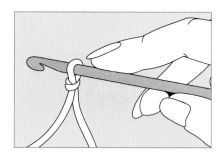

YARN OVER

Bring the yarn over the top of the hook from **back** to **front**, catching the yarn with the hook and turning the hook slightly toward you to keep the yarn from slipping off *(Fig. 9)*.

Fig. 9

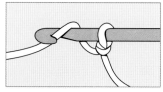

CHAIN

Yarn over *(Fig. 9)*, draw the yarn through the loop on the hook *(Fig. 10)*.

Fig. 10

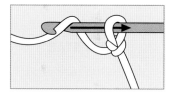

SLIP STITCH

Insert hook in stitch indicated, yarn over and draw through stitch and loop on the hook *(Fig. 11)*.

Fig. 11

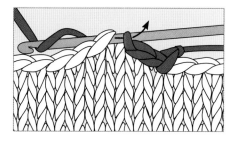

Yarn Information

The blankets and cocoons in this book were made using a variety of yarn weights. Any brand of the specified weight of yarn may be used. It is best to refer to the yardage/meters when determining how many skeins or balls to purchase. Remember, to arrive at the finished size, it is the GAUGE/TENSION that is important, not the brand of yarn.

For your convenience, listed below are the yarns used to create our photography models. Because yarn manufacturers make frequent changes in their product lines, you may sometimes find it necessary to use a substitute yarn or to search for the discontinued product at alternate suppliers (locally or online).

RAINBOW BLOCKS

Red Heart® Anne Geddes Baby™

Red - #902 Ladybug

Light Yellow - #203 Daffodil

Yellow - #226 Bumble

Green - #691 Grass

Orange - #261 Tangerine

Blue - #827 Bluejay

QUILT STAR

Lion Brand® Babysoft®

Print - #293 Twinkle Print

Blue - #107 Bluebell

Light Blue - #106 Pastel Blue

BORDERED SQUARE

Patons® Beehive Baby Chunky™

#76233 Quicker Clover

BASKETWEAVE

Lion Brand® Babysoft®

#143 Lavender

RIPPLES

Patons® Astra™

Yellow - #02941 School Bus Yellow

Light Yellow - #02943 Maize Yellow

HEXAGONS

Lion Brand® Babysoft®

Pink - #101 Pastel Pink

Yellow - #157 Pastel Yellow

Green - #156 Pastel Green

BUNNY COCOON & HAT

Red Heart® Buttercup®

Print - #4935 Aqua Ice

Red Heart® Soft Baby Steps®

White - #9600 White

HOODED COCOON

Bernat® Baby Blanket™

#04616 Pitter Patter

We have made every effort to ensure that these instructions are accurate and complete. We cannot, however, be responsible for human error, typographical mistakes, or variations in individual work.

Production Team: Instructional/Technical Writer - Cathy Hardy; Editorial Writer - Susan Frantz Wiles; Senior Graphic Artist - Lora Puls; Graphic Artist - Victoria Temple; Photo Stylist - Lori Wenger; and Photographers - Jason Masters and Ken West.